All Scripture references taken from the KJV of the Holy Bible unless otherwise indicated.

TOXIC SOULS, Book 2 of 3 from

The Upgrade Series

Freshwater Press, USA

Dr. Marlene Miles

ISBN: 978-1-960150-34-9

Paperback Version

Copyright 2023

All Rights reserved. No part of this book may be reproduced, distributed or transmitted by any means or in any means including photocopying, recording or other electronic or mechanical methods without prior written permission of the publisher except in the case of brief publications or critical reviews.

Table of Contents

Upgrade 4
What Colors The Soul? 9
How To? 13
Gratification 17
Innocence 20
Where Are You? 22
Big 24
New Spirit 31
Escape 34
Dinah's Toxic Brothers 37
Tell Me How 42
You Should Have Forgiven 49
Hungry Versus Happy 50
Do Not Curse 52
Consider This 57
Let It Be Done 61
It Is Finished 67
By Faith 70
Toxic Parents 74
Jesus Wasn't Toxic 80
Dear Reader: 84
Books in this series 85
Christian books by this author: 86

UPGRADE SERIES

Book 2

TOXIC SOULS

Freshwater Press

USA

Upgrade

This book is for grown people. It is not racy or offensive, but it is for adults versus the children of adults. This title, **Toxic Souls** is Book 2 from the Upgrade Series which has three books in it.

I must say: I love kids. Don't get me wrong about that. I love kids, but don't talk to me about the *innocence* of children.

Babies come here in *survival mode.* They have to; they don't have a choice. Once here, they are at the mercy of every adult, every person who's bigger than they are during their infanthood, childhood, and sometimes beyond if they find themselves in a predatorial environment. The Me-too's and many other abuse victims can unfortunately vouch that there are predators in this world.

From their arrival, babies and toddlers are at the mercy of every hand that feeds them, carries them, or even plays with them. In that caregiving, there can be a lot of love, or there can be assaults, hurts, or a lot of threats, depending on what type of situation that child is born into.

The little *souls* of babies are not prospered either. A prospered soul is calm, it trusts its environment and the process of life.

Because of being at the mercy of everything and everyone around them, until babies know it's safe, or learn to trust their environment and their caregivers, they are in survival mode. All of us were when we arrived on this planet.

As we age and get bigger, more able to speak up for ourselves, more able to defend ourselves, if necessary. Eventually, we become more able to navigate life. In all this growing, if we don't prosper our souls because we *can't,* or we are thwarted from growing because of a toxic environment, or we just don't intend to grow up--, we just won't have a prospered soul.

As we grow and age we should mature emotionally, as well. We should be maturing in the things of God if we call ourselves Christians because we have a mandate to grow up and also prosper our souls as in, 2 Thessalonians 5:23, and 2 Thessalonians 4:4. So spiritual, soul and physical growth is a mandate.

Babies and children can have it rough--, until they know what they're born into, until they know what they've gotten as a family, and as a community. Until they realize that their environment is safe and conducive for thriving and growing, they are in survival mode. That may be true for some children and also, it's true for some adults, as well. To be born into circumstances or situations that keep your soul from flourishing and prospering can be hidden from a child, because he has no point of reference, no real understanding of what he has been born into. What he has, what he lives each day is all he or she knows, so it's their *normal*.

It may not be until years later with proper socialization that they realize that they were born into or raised in unfortunate circumstances that may **not** have been *normal*. Perhaps their living situation was not optimum for the growth and development of trust and peace and even happiness. The situation that they were born into may not have prospered their soul; it may have done the exact opposite.

What Colors The Soul?

In any relationship, especially a child-to-adult relationship, the child has to learn to trust that adult if for no reason than the sheer size of the adult. Trust must be **learned** if it is not instilled in us by God at the onset of any connection. Have you noticed that even babies will connect easily with some people while with others the child may cry or run away instinctively, sensing danger. That is, after the child is mobile and can run. Before that, there is a lot of crying when a baby instinctively does not like a person.

What we all go through, especially as children *colors* our souls. The more intense the event or the perception and impression of the event, the deeper and longer lasting will be the imprint and the impact on that soul.

What we go through in life, especially as children, can either comfort and grow us up and usher us into trust or do the very opposite and push us deeper into *survival mode*. We know survival mode, from the first book of this series, **Upgrade, How To Get Out of Survival Mode**, is a stress mode, a flesh mode, emergency mode, and it's not where we want to be; it is not the ideal for civilized living.

Parents must protect, nurture and care for their children and teach them to trust the environment, their siblings, the entire family and ultimately, the whole world that they've been born into. Else you have a timid, on-edge child who will not thrive emotionally, or socially.

It is not always *just* what happens to a child, it is what has happened to the child's parents and caregivers that they've never resolved or gotten over. *Baggage,* it's called; and it is not just in interpersonal relationships. What you've been through in life and your perception and memories of it have colored your soul.

Parents are adept at casting their own fears on their children, while at the same time continuing to harbor and perhaps grow those fears, in themselves.

As a dentist, I have to keep the fearful parents **out** of the treatment room of their children – especially the younger children who haven't formulated their own opinion of dental care yet. Parents most often don't get it; they think they are *protecting* their children, but that *spirit of fear* tries to take over the room.

That's at the office and in the treatment room. We only find out later how much absolutely fearful and wrong *STUFF* the parent has said to this child, before the dental appointment, in the name of love. The parent is trying to prepare the child, basically by scaring the child, without even realizing it.

Then we find out later how much stuff has been said, prior to the dental visit, by the siblings, sometimes in jest, but many times, also in fear to perpetuate fear in this entire fearful family. It is self-fulfilling prophecy. This family is so afraid that they avoid the care they need and end up having the worst dental needs and outcomes possible.

How To?

Without God, how will we know exactly what kind of care and nurture to offer a baby or a child? What is enough? What is too much? Every child is different. Everyone needs to be ministered to differently. Parents of multiple children know exactly what I'm talking about. There's no such thing as a cookie cutter kid.

If you're lucky enough to get a child that is **you**--, so much you that you know exactly how to minister to them, thank God. Still, you may not really know until years or decades later if you were right.

There are two parents, two sets of chromosomes coming together. There are two cultures, two backgrounds, at least two family *altars*, two bloodlines. Neither is the *only* parent, neither parent is the only one contributing to the genetic and spiritual makeup of the baby.

So, here's your darling baby born into survival mode. Thankfully it's not as dire as being born in a barn and put in the animal's feeding trough, but it **is** survival mode, nonetheless.

In survival mode, your baby learns:

- Cry--. Feed me.
- Cry, change me.
- Cry, pick me up. Cry.

- Cry, something hurts.

Not having a language begins the difficult journey, although the parents, if they are good parents, are working overtime to make it as comfortable and as bearable for the little one as possible.

This beginning teaches the child a selfish, me-centered, flesh-centered survival focus. Nonverbally, the tot may be thinking, *How will they know what I need if I don't make noise?* You know, the squeaky wheel gets the oil. Babies complain very loudly and wow, it works, they get what they want. This leads them to become self-centered.

Then, it's one or two or three more years with no real language skills or very weak language skills until a child really learns to communicate. Some adults never perfect communication for whatever reason, some out of plain laziness.

So, in the years where your child has not really been able to speak, based on the interactions they've had with parents, siblings, pets, relatives, and other babies and toddlers, **what have they internalized?**

We don't know, do we?

Whatever has happened to them in these first years is the stuff that has helped to color their **SOUL**.

Gratification

No one can deny that we have to attend to the needs of a baby immediately, which teaches immediate gratification. A person could get used to that. A baby does get used to it, and that immediate gratification, giving them what they need or what they cry for, what you think they need, to make them *happy* makes them believe that this is how life works.

No wonder they are found cooing and singing in their cribs in the middle of the night. They may be thinking, *My environment is good. These big people serve me; I get what I want: this is great!*

Just because your child is happy (right now) doesn't mean that their soul is prospering. Happy can be fleeting, and what does a baby know of soul prosperity? A baby just knows if its flesh needs, and desires are met or not. And they can complain loudly when they are not met.

Right now.

As a matter of fact, immediate gratification, the very thing that makes people *happy* teaches the **opposite** of soul prosperity. *Happy* is not the measure. Although most parents say that they want their child to be happy.

Who wouldn't be happy as long as they are getting everything they want?

As they grow older, children start to develop emotions that they *can* express. They can become jealous, for example. They cry when it's their little friend's birthday and they **also** don't get a gift or a cake--, or, a gift *and* a cake. After all they are used to being the center of attention and getting everything. They may be wondering why is all this changing. *Why am I not still getting EVERYTHING?*

Innocence

So, you tell me, is that innocence? Is it? You tell me. Children can be violent. How many fights do you have to break up between kids? Even siblings--, maybe and especially between siblings? Is that innocence? Kids take what they want, when they want. They take toys, cookies--, whatever. They sneak, they steal.

A child has to be taught to be nice, play nice, and be civil. Else, have you noticed that they behave as if they are in survival mode? They are fervent after what they think they need to survive; that does not have to be taught to them. Rather, it has to be untaught.

What you have to teach your children is *delayed gratification* and that is a huge part of soul prosperity. We all have to learn that, or we become (or stay) needy, greedy, self-centered people.

Children want what they want, when they want it. Most often it's now; spoiled adults are the same way. Children want pretty much everything they see, and they want it **now**. That's flesh. That is all flesh.

In adults, that's toxic. That is a toxic soul.

Where Are You?

Toxic souls are always scheming and screaming and scamming to get stuff by any means. The adult who's like that is far more dangerous than a child because the adult now has language. He has language skills to use in controlling others, manipulating others, guilt tripping, dominating, or gaslighting others. As important, this adult now has size, ability and power.

He has power, such as money.

An unprospered, toxic soul will hide when they get caught, just as children often do. They hide when they take things, for example.

We can hear modern day parents say, *It's OK, Junior. Tell us what you did. You're not going to get in trouble. Just tell me the truth.*

*How a*re you talking to an *innocent* when you have to coax a **confession** out of them? You let me know. You may argue that the child didn't know any better. Then why did the child know to *hide*?

Adam and Eve, in the Garden, sinned, and then hid.

Big

But the children whose souls are still unprospered--, their bodies haven't gotten tall enough, big enough to do the stuff they probably **really** want to do, yet, you know, the *other stuff* that is considered to make them *not innocent*, but **guilty**? Could this be why they come here tiny and helpless? So they can be taught how to do right before they get to an adult size where they can *really* do what they *want* to do?

Anyhow, we're supposed to believe that children come here innocent and then somehow, they *become* guilty? How? *When*? When does that happen? **No, they came here just like that.** If they are not in an environment that allows their little souls to grow and prosper, to feel safe and trust, they can stay just like that, or become worse.

Like David we were all **conceived in sin and shapen in iniquity,** (Psalm 51).

Sadly, soberly, we humans come here un-innocent and without Jesus onboard and by help of the Holy Spirit, it gets worse day by day.

Power shows everyone exactly who you are. It's when we get big enough, tall enough and have ability enough, money enough, when we get power, the **big reveal** happens. That's when we reveal who we really are by our deeds, in our actions. By our fruit, we will be known.

So back to kids because you were once one--.

What is it that corrupts them if they come here so *innocent*? Or do they just become un-innocent when they meet those *other kids* at school and daycare? You know, the kids that corrupt your child. You know I'm not talking about your kid, right? I'm talking about those *other* kids.

So kids know how to be selfish. They know how to cry for everything they want. They know how to hit people. Even you. They bite. They know how to lie to try to get out of trouble.

Come on, your child wouldn't need to be taught and trained and taught and trained if they were so innocent. Children have to be told everything over and over again. Kids will try you. Even when you know that you've taught them better, they still try you, to do and to get exactly what they want. Children can be very self-willed and in a child, that's called childish, but in an adult that's what I call **toxic**. It is the trait of an unprospered soul to have the *will* running things.

That's a toxic soul.

Now they've gotten big enough, they have power, they have enough money to do what they want, you'll see who they really are. They will show you their souls, and that soul will either be well-ordered and prosperous, or it will be toxic.

If we are all born so innocent, why is it that human nature is the stuff that gets us into trouble with God? It's because human nature is sin nature. So you and I both know I have not only described children, but also *childishness* in adults.

Childish adults are toxic. They're immature, and we call them childish. But we wouldn't call them childish if childish was innocent. If they were innocent, why wouldn't they be called adults? No, they're called childish, and big people who haven't prospered in their souls, those who haven't grown up, are toxic. They have toxic souls, and nobody really wants to be around that.

It can be dangerous to deal with them, actually, but some of them learn to hide their toxicity and trick others into being around them--, or giving them what they want.

They have toxic souls.

The difference here is that in kids, their little souls, are unprospered when they get here. They must be taught and nurtured into growing up and led into prospering their soul. It's the kid's choice, ultimately. It's full-time work for the parents, who have to nudge, coach, teach, sometimes preach to their kids to get them to grow up.

Kids, to me, aren't toxic unless they willfully decide not to grow up, especially if they try to *hide* the fact that they are defiantly not growing up and still insisting on their own way.

But adults who should know better are toxic. Adults are toxic because they are unprospered in their souls and they know it, but they use flesh and devilish tactics to cover their immaturity. Adults who are tall enough, and big enough to do the stuff they really want to do, and they know better, are toxic. The other stuff that they consider that makes them innocent, but not guilty, still makes them toxic.

Oh, they don't want to grow up. They are Toys R Us kids. Notice how that business model didn't even work. Toys R Us is closed. Not growing up is not a viable option, Peter Pan, it doesn't work. We have to grow. We must grow in the natural and we have to grow spiritually and mature in the things of God.

Kids are simply unprospered in their souls. They just got here so we give them a break. There's hope with adults around, there's a chance that they are still under their parents care, teaching, and tutelage.

New Spirit

Kids will grow even without Jesus. But until they know Jesus, they most likely won't grow the right way.

But adults, **with** Jesus, when we get saved, our spirit is made new. So it's up to us to prosper our souls, to grow up, and to be mentally, emotionally and intellectually matured. That is the next **upgrade** for us.

So, the souls of grown folks depend on what they've been through in life, including their childhoods, including their childhood issues *that may not be resolved yet.* It also depends on how and if they've been taught to handle their emotions. But you see, Jesus restores your soul.

He restores my soul, (Psalm 23).

We ask God to restore our souls, restore us back to where we were when we first were made by Him, because He made us good. He made us and He said that is good. Then He blessed us.

We need to get back to when we first trusted God, and we trusted life –if we ever have. We need to ask God to recover us and deliver us from all of the things we may need to be delivered from.

Born in the nature of Adam, and that's a sin nature. Adam did what in the garden? He sinned.

And after that, what did he do? He hid.

And, after that, he did what? He lied.

I usually say here that he blamed EVE, but really Adam blamed God. That's some serious toxicity.

Sin nature is to blame someone else, anyone else to get out of trouble; it is to lie. But if we're all born Innocent, then why do we automatically sin? Why do we automatically hide? Why do we automatically lie? Why do we need to get saved?

Because we're not born innocent, we're born in sin nature. Some aren't born into sin, ALL of us are. Even the pretty babies, the cute babies, the adorable babies. Even you. Even your children.

Sorry.

Escape

So don't talk to me about the innocence of children. Even a baby will give you the side eye if you're not doing what they want. Babies may not be guilty of crimes or sins, but they have *desires.* They have desires to do things as soon as they can break out of that playpen, as soon as they can break out of that crib. And you know that they are forever trying to escape, out of playpens, out of cribs, out of houses, away from holding your hand in stores. You have to keep your eye on them or go look for them as soon as you lose sight of them.

Just because your kid can't talk yet doesn't make them innocent. Just because they haven't learned the language yet doesn't make them innocent. Just because they smile a lot and haven't started teething yet, which is generally when they start getting cranky, that doesn't make them innocent.

So you see, the only reason they are not worse is because they're still too little. I'm pretty sure that's why God doesn't give power to babies and kids. What may be in their minds, if they were big enough to do it, can be told in the *childish* adult whose mind/soul never prospers and he gets power and begins to do heinous things.

Power is probably exactly what a baby or a kid wants. They want power. They want to be superheroes. They want power. Most don't want to create happily ever after's, they want to do things to people that they perceive have done, or are doing things to them – UNTIL and unless you teach them better.

And you must teach them that over and over again to offset what they are really thinking, or what the enemy is whispering to them 24/7.

Of course you know money is power. And that could be why God doesn't give money to immature and childish people. Because they'll wreak havoc with it.

Pray that the Lord will prosper your soul. Pray and do the work to have a prospered soul and come out of toxicity.

Now, I want to tell a couple of stories…

Dinah's Toxic Brothers

There's a story about 10 toxic adults in Genesis 37, Jacob's 10 boys put their brother Joseph in a well and sold him into slavery. Then they told their father that a wild animal had killed Joseph. This grieved the old man, but those ten didn't seem to have a conscience about that, they didn't care that they stressed their dad almost to a breaking point. They didn't care, as long as they did what they wanted, and got the outcome that they thought they wanted. Just like immature, unprospered souls.

This is a toxic behavior but is it really **not** a surprise since earlier in Genesis the same boys in Chapter 34, exacted their version of revenge after their only sister Dinah was sexually assaulted. These same boys, or I should say they were adult men at that time, devised the scheme to kill the man who assaulted Dinah and also to kill that man's father.

Even though the man apologized and wanted to marry Dinah and bring dowry or offerings to Jacob, to try to make it right, the Brothers did not accept that. The boys wouldn't agree with that, but came up with another plan of their own. Of course, we know from Genesis 34 the plans of these 10 men are diabolical, murderous, and contemptible. If they did that to their own BROTHER – Lord have mercy on anyone else that they would scheme against.

So these 10 men said, *"Hey, why not lie to these people. Let's trick all the men in the whole city and get them to circumcise themselves."* So they started a campaign and soon they had accomplished a great mass circumcision where all the men in that city were circumcised. Then, on the third day, which they say is the worst day after circumcision, they attacked and killed all the men in the whole city. Then they took all the women and all the children back to their own city as slaves.

This is an example of the response that unprospered, toxic souls will make to hurts, slights, and perceived slights. Yes, the rape of Dinah was horrendous, but does it balance with the murder of **all** the men of a city? ALL the men didn't rape her.

Does it jibe with the taking of all the women and children into captivity for slavery? NONE of the women or children of that city had raped Dinah. An unprospered soul, with unchecked power, means, and ability, will have an over-the-top response to an assault or a trauma.

Recall these 10 grown men were traumatized by Joseph who did nothing to them really. Joseph did nothing but:

1. Be his father's favorite.

2. Have an amazing dream and destiny from God. So it was obvious that Joseph was one of God's favorites, too.

Beloved, I pray above all things that you would prosper and be in health, even as your soul prospers. Could it be that God is withholding power, wealth, money, and finances from souls who aren't prospered because God knows what they would do with all the power, wealth, and money???

Of course. That's why soul prosperity is a prerequisite of receiving certain blessings from God.

Tell Me How

So how do you prosper in your soul? Well, the first tenant of Christianity is forgiveness. If you can't do that, then you need to go back to the beginning, when you first say you believed.

Forgiveness is first because it is what Jesus did for us. And, because the perceived hurts, the real hurt, and the memories of unresolved issues, and unhealed hurts most often need to be **forgiven**.

Wrongs done to us from when we were kids usually foster revenge plots, thoughts of vengeance, and payback plans. We may think of stuff we want to do to people--, either to actually do things to them, or to do something that's over the top to *show them* that they **didn't** hurt us, which is still really revenge.

But if we forgive, we don't have that potential sin knocking at the door, as a temptation. So forgiveness is the first thing, the first tenant of Christianity. You prosper in your soul by next asking God to restore your soul. Always seek the truth of a matter, knowledge and Wisdom to know how to use that knowledge. You become God-focused and encourage yourself in the Lord. And, in all your getting, get understanding. Get your soul reset by God back to **before** the incident that you need to forgive.

Practice patience. Delayed gratification teaches patience. Practice one-another ministry; love your neighbor as yourself and be good to one another. Be thankful; practice gratitude. Share. Be joyful, be kind. Move in the Fruits of the Spirit and turn away from the works of the flesh.

But if you're a parent, you also have to learn how to prosper your child's soul, or at least lead them in the way toward soul prosperity so they don't become a toxic adult. Do this the same way you'd do for yourself. Don't forget how you grew up and what affected you favorably, what didn't affect you favorably, and teach your children the virtues of godliness.

Children don't know a lot, so don't laugh at them or with them when they're wrong. Sometimes the stuff they do is hilarious, but you can't always let them see you laughing at their mistakes, this it could hurt their feelings, or it could teach them to be silly--, too silly, or silly too often.

Don't condone bad behavior unless you want them to keep repeating it. Using cuss words comes to mind, too many parents think that's funny. Once this is accepted in the house your kid will take it to school and get in trouble with the teacher and the principal. He will take it to grandma's house, and to church and embarrass you quite a bit.

Of note, I just learned this week that using foul language and a lot of curse words is a sign of being a *captive soul*.

See parents, instead of laughing, you need to be praying and rescuing your darling(s) from captivity. Maybe only a little of their soul was stolen and held captive – for now. Perhaps it is the beginning of the planned destruction of your child.

Parents, having children is not for the faint of heart. It is non-stop, 24/7 if you are going to do it right.

Laughing at your children, even though what they do is funny, it is not expedient when you should be teaching them and not using them for your entertainment. Your children won't learn anything if you do that, and they won't respect you in the long run. If you do that, that is how you've demoted yourself to their level, giving up your parental authority.

Teach your children at all times.

Parents, this is where I say this is for grown people, because you cannot be friends with your children until they are mature. Making your child your peer, your equal, or your friend, while they're young and immature is usually a mistake.

Can you go over to your neighbor's house and be best friends with their toddler? Of course not. This sounds ridiculous, doesn't it? You see, grown people and babies are not best friends. The immature cannot be parentized and the parents should not act like teenagers, even if it's fun or you're desperately trying to stay young--, you can't do it.

You keep trying it and it really doesn't work. Perhaps it's what you wanted as a child, for your parent to be your friend so you can do what they did, see what the big people saw, and eat what they ate, and drink what they drink, and stay up late. So now you've decided to offer that to your child. That's a mistake. It doesn't work.

It is a sign that you have an unprospered soul. Further, as you are to walk in dominion and have authority over your house, your family and be the watchman for them, if you've relinquished your authority to anyone, the devil, a stranger, your child--, how will you stand in authority and decree and declare? You will have given up your authority, influence and power to pray for them. Not only is that not helping anyone, it is a most hurtful thing to do, spiritually speaking. To leave your child and family unprotected, spiritually because you are not walking in your God-given authority is not smart or caring.

You Should Have Forgiven

Because you should have already put childish things away by now, you should have already forgiven your parents of perceived hurts and real hurts. So, by the time you have children, your childish wishes and what should have been have been settled. Those issues should have been healed already. This way, they will not bleed over into your new family. A child should not suffer because of your soul's issues and unhealed hurts and emotions. Even if your parents didn't do it for you, even if they couldn't, do it for your children.

Hungry Versus Happy

Balance is the critical thing. Don't spoil a child by giving them everything they want. Your child's soul is not prospered so they will want unprospered things--, namely everything they see, except spinach and onions.

A soul comes here hungry. When a person is grown, and they are still hungry that is a sign of an unprospered soul. Some describe their hunger as greediness—okay they are greedy. Remember, immediate gratification works *against* soul prosperity.

Even if your child is *happy*, they still could be an unprospered, toxic soul.

But I also want you to hear this thing.

Do Not Curse

Do not curse your children. Do not curse your bloodline. I don't mean using curse or cuss words but speaking *curses* over your children, but don't do that either. In the Book of Numbers it says that what God has blessed no man can curse and what God has cursed, no man can bless. Still, Heaven and Earth have to agree for some things to happen in the Earth.

Sometimes people, in anger and error, while they're in the flesh, agree with the devil. They may not mean to agree with the devil, but that's what they are doing.

Do not curse your children or speak curses over them.

What am I talking about?

Never tell a child or any person you know that they are worthless or won't amount to anything. Do not tell your child they're no good. Do not tell a child that they are stupid or dumb or ugly or lazy. Do not tell your child that you're sorry they were born. Do not downgrade or degrade your child.

Children and most adults don't understand this kind of talk. What you *think* is reverse psychology is not that at all. It is devastating. They will not do the opposite of the negative thing that you just spoke over them just to prove you wrong.

Sometimes they can't.

Sometimes your evil, negative words are crippling to them. If you and your word carries a lot of authority over a person (especially minor children and *your* children) when your words are so grievous and hateful, it may oppress your child and render them helpless and hopeless.

For life.

If not for life, for a long time.

And it shows you are toxic.

Your words are word curses so your, impressionable minds and souls cannot even overcome those words to succeed in life. What God has blessed, no man can curse. Has God already blessed your child?

Your young, minor child may not be at the age of accountability yet. Your child may not have received Salvation and accepted Jesus as their Lord and Savior yet. Why in the world would you speak damning words over them, over their life, to curse them? Your curse will stand if God has not already blessed them.

If God has already blessed them and you're trying to curse them, they are protected from *you*. Why would God have to protect your child from *you*? What kind of parent are you? Why would God have to protect any child from his parent?

Because sometimes parents are the worse things that can happen to a child.

Pray to the Lord that you are not that toxic parent with your own unprospered soul, especially if you have a minor child who has their own soul that needs to prosper. The child is counting on you, but you are ill-equipped to minister to them if you have not matured yourself. Such behavior is what identifies a toxic parent.

Further, when a curse is uttered knowingly, or unknowingly, if it does not alight on the intended victim, it is coming back on the one who uttered it. If you utter a curse against anyone, even your own family member or child, and they are blessed by God and protected by God, get ready for that stone to roll back on you.

Consider This

Consider this, because you've been through it yourself in your own life, you know that your child will have enough people--, maybe too many people working against them and speaking against them, competing against them in schools, in the workplace, in the world--, for their entire life.

At home, especially growing up, their childhood should be a safe place, a haven where they're built up, not a place of more warfare. Even a soldier must rest sometime. Your minor child is not a soldier. If you don't have anything positive and uplifting to say to, over, or about your child--, say nothing.

Nothing.

I wrote a very short, illustrated book about this entitled, **Don't Say That To Me**. https://a.co/d/0uJLDds

Your cute, sweet, seemingly innocent child can grow up to be a loaded weapon. He or she will represent you to God in two or three generations to determine if *you've* done a good job or not.

Don't let your child be your undoing. Don't let your child's childhood be *their* undoing. Because you love your child, don't spoil them. Don't let your child's childhood be so traumatic and grievous that it is their undoing. Your child's undoing could be your undoing, or the undoing of your family or your entire family's bloodline because God will be *visiting*.

Be good to your children but balanced. Train them up in the way they should go. Teach them at all times. Do not oppress or be burdensome to your children. Pray for their future. Equip them to have good successes in life. Bless them.

Don't be a toxic soul yourself. Ask the Lord to restore and heal your soul. I pray that you do not hinder the growth of your child's soul or put stumbling blocks on their road to soul prosperity.

I pray the Lord restore *your* soul from all childishness, unhealed hurts, unmet needs, and toxicity and that you will be in health and prosper, even as your soul prospers. This will be a serious upgrade to you. When you upgrade your children, you upgrade yourself, through your generations and bloodline.

Let It Be Done

And Jesus taught His Disciples how to pray. From the King James, we read:

Thy Kingdom come, thy will be done in Earth as it is in Heaven, (Matthew 6:10).

I have brought you glory on Earth by finishing the work you gave me to do.
(John 17:4 NIV)

That is Jesus speaking, so our job is to find out what's happening in Heaven. We need to find out what has already happened in Heaven. Find out what's been *done* in Heaven, because we want the will of God that is in Heaven to be done also in Earth.

Okay, what is happening in Heaven? What has happened? What has God already *done*? What has already been completed in Heaven?

We also need to find out what God has said about us, what God has said about you, about me, already. Then we agree with God, agree with Heaven. Agree, so that Heaven and Earth--, Heaven and earthen vessels, *that's us---*, agree. So things will *be done.*

Let it be done. Do you realize that nothing in the Earth resists the will of God?

Except man.

So what's wrong with us? What is wrong with man? He does have free will, but nothing else resists the will of God. Nothing else resists

God. Nothing. Not the sun, not the moon, not the oceans, not the mountains, not plants or animals resist the Lord, except, that fig tree that Jesus cursed because it did not bear fruit.

Even at the Name of Jesus every knee must bow – so that means that the Devil is afraid of God, the Name of Jesus and the Blood of Jesus.

What is wrong with man?

Nothing else resists God or the Spirit of God.

This Upgrade Series is a serious challenge to the reset of your life.

As we come out of wrong thinking and out of survival mode, we come out of the flesh, and we begin to mature spiritually.

Survival mode as we recall from Book 1 of the Upgrade series, **Upgrade: How to Get**

Out of Survival Mode, survival mode is emergency mode. It is a flesh mode. It is so right now because the flesh wants what it sees right now. The flesh wants what it heard about, what it tasted, what it smelled, what it *felt*. The flesh wants some **more**.

In the Earth, our five senses want to run the show. The flesh wants to run you, but 1 Corinthians 1:29 says that no flesh shall glory in God's presence. There's no real reason to build your flesh up, it's not leaving the planet, but your spirit and your soul are eternal.

Jesus brought glory to God by doing the work that God sent Him here to do. So can we. So should we. No flesh will glory in Heaven because your flesh, my flesh, is not getting into Heaven.

You see, the purpose of being on Earth is to be spiritual, *while* in a flesh body. Earth is a testing ground, a proving ground, if you will. So being all flesh while in a flesh body, well, how hard is that? That's only natural.

Why would Jesus need to come to Earth, die a horrible death on a cross by crucifixion, for that? For us to continue to be all flesh in a flesh body for us to continue in our sin? No, He wouldn't; if we are changing nothing, then that would have been unnecessary.

To stay in the flesh is the path of least resistance; flesh is a downgrade from the soul and spirit. To ascend at least to soul prosperity is the upgrade. To transcend and walk by the Spirit is reason for Jesus' work here on Earth and at Calvary. It is how we will prosper and receive the Kingdom.

Now we have grown a bit, we have prospered in our souls a bit, we leave off working the flesh. *Right*?

We've transcended all that emergency survival flesh stuff. We've prospered our souls and we've moved into soul prosperity. As we've aspired to and ascended to the NOW of God, we then find out what's happening in Heaven, or more like what's *already happened*, because it is **finished**. In God's now we have been fully upgraded.

To walk in God's NOW is the maximum upgrade.

It Is Finished

It is finished. The work is finished. Walk in it. If you have great faith, while in the Earth, you can walk in what's already been done in Heaven. Earth is our great test of faith. God transcends all space and time. Shouldn't we be more like Him by now? We should be praying from the place where God says we are already. We are *already* healed. We are already whole.

We are already prosperous. We should be praying from the place where God is, and we should be dealing in God's **NOW** instead of our now. We should be praying like Jesus, from the place of completion, from the place of *finished*, from the place of *done*.

It is done; put a fork in it. Set the table. Maybe that's why God prepares the table even in the presence of your enemies, because ***it's already done***.

The enemies can roll up if they dare, but there's not much they can do to mess this up as long as we are in faith and we believe, walk, and talk like everything is already done.

Remember, also our *now* is the ***now*** of our senses and our symptoms, our worries, our fears and our problems. But we are spiritual beings, having a flesh experience and the flesh is so now. *I think, I want, I feel, I hear, I see.*

But God's **NOW** is the *it is finished NOW*, where everything that God says we are, we are. Everything God says we have, we have.

In His NOW, God sees the perfected you--, where *it is done*. The perfected you has a prospered, well-ordered soul, not a toxic one.

That's probably why God can stand any of us. It's probably why His Mercy endures, because God is looking at the **finished** one of any of us. He's not looking at the survival mode you, or the flesh mode me, or the petty mode anybody else, or the foolish things that we might be from day-to-day.

By Faith

God uses faith. That's why He's challenging us, because without faith it is impossible to please God. Let it be done on Earth as it is done in Heaven. The first part of that is God's Will *will* be done. Some of us may think that God's Will may be whatever mood He's in this morning, but no, it's not even like that. But if it were, it would be okay because God is Supreme. He is the Most High God.

As before stated, nothing resists the will of God except man—foolish, disobedient, rebellious man. We needn't be so stupid, so foolish. Nothing resists Him--, not the Earth, not the stars, not the sun, not the moon.

Everything obeys His command, so ***it is done*** means everything is completed already. It's not up to a whimsical, mercurial, moody God. He is not that way; God is the same today, forever (Hebrews 13:7).

It is already done, and the Word, *done* in this verse is not just the manner in which something is accomplished, but it means ***that*** it is already accomplished. It is already done. It is already finished. It is completed, it has *become*. It has come into existence. It be; it is. It has come to pass. It has happened. It is made. It is finished. God is saying it's already done. Jesus said He has finished the work.

When Jesus taught the Disciples to pray. He said, **Pray thusly, thy will be done on Earth as it is in Heaven.** *Done. Finished.* And, in the volume of the Book where it's written about you, it's already written, (Psalms 40:7). It's done. Glory to God, you're in The Book. I'm in The Book, we're in it. The Lamb's Book of Life.

We are in The Book as *what*? Why did we come here? It is not so we could carve our names on a tree and say we were here. It is not just to keep our bloodline name in the Earth, although that is part of why we come here. Our name is written in The Book to tell our story and what part we played in the Will of God. It is to tell how we dressed the Garden. It is to tell how we subdued the Earth. It is written in that Book to tell how we were fruitful and multiplied.

Our name is written in The Book for reasons that will teach others and inspire others. Our story is there to tell of the exploits we did in the Earth because we know Our God. Our story should include how we, like Jesus destroyed the works of the Devil while we walked among men.

Our names are not just written in The Book for roll call.

Toxic Parents

Mistakenly a lot of kids think that they have toxic parents because the kid's definition of toxic is having too many rules and requirements. Toxic can be described as one who is always negative and stress-inducing. That might be true of rules to a kid, but that should not be the intent of family structure and order in the home.

The toxic person is someone who has not prospered in their soul. Having an unprospered soul means the person is still childish and greedy. Toxic people are manipulators. They are a little creepy in that you feel uncomfortable or bad around them. They throw shade and make innuendos and do things that you that they should apologize to you about, but they never do.

They are not clear in motives or purpose and leave you guessing and confused. They are hit or miss; they are terribly inconsistent.

They don't respect you or your boundaries, but insist on theirs being honored. *"No, don't call my house after 9pm."* Really? But when they want your attention, they want all of it, they are kind of narcissistic and demanding. And the drama--, don't forget the drama.

Women, have I described half the men you've dated? Those types are *scared* to enter into relationship with you; they are afraid to commit. They probably don't know *how* to commit.

They are not a "Playa", **they are toxic.**

You need a serious upgrade in the quality and type of men you date. In your dating life look for men with prospered souls. They can't just be good looking or have a nice career; look for prospered souls.

Don't make excuses for him anymore than you'd make them for yourself.

Having a toxic soul as an adult could mean that the person was traumatized and has not healed, recovered, been delivered or restored from those traumas. Discern if you're dating someone who wants to be healed of their traumas, or if they want to meet someone who will **let them continue to have their damaged soul** because either that's all they know, or it's convenient for them. If you ever hear or sense, *"That's the way I am and I'm not changing"* --, RUN!

Hurt or trauma can freeze a person in that place and time, and they don't even realize that they are stuck. They are stuck because they are captive, bound. In that particular trauma, the devil either TOOK a piece of their soul, or they willingly gave it up, saying something like, *"I'm never going to forgive so and so."*

It makes sense that they want and need all this attention, because they really are having a serious spiritual problem if their soul is captive. They need help, but unless they are willing and ready to come out of captivity, AND God *sent* you to go get them, you will be spinning your wheels.

People who are captive or stuck, are fortunate when God sends someone to go get them. When God sends someone to go get a soul out of lockdown, that is called deliverance.

Often, someone has to tell the captive that they are *stuck*. If it's your own child--, well in the mouth of babes, God has ordained praise. If God can speak through a donkey, He can certainly speak through young people. However, just because your child is complaining that you're toxic, doesn't make it true. They may just want you to lighten up on the rules so they can be "happy" and do as they please.

Ask God, for your sake and for theirs.

You want to be fully delivered yourself and you want to minister to your child properly, so they don't grow up still unprospered and toxic.

Jesus Wasn't Toxic

You can't afford to be toxic and unprospered in your soul; Jesus wasn't.

Soul toxicity hinders our Christian walk and ministry. Jesus said, **He has nothing in Me.** That should be our goal as well, that the devil have nothing on us and no hooks in us. We need to be free to live life and do our ministry.

Jesus stressed the demons out, but Jesus is Peace. Jesus is Love. The Spirit of Jesus brings, fulness of Joy. The angels said, Peace on Earth and goodwill to all **men**. The fullness of the Fruit of the Spirit is the Holy Spirit—that Spirit is God's Spirit, which Christ left for us at the Day of Pentecost.

Jesus did not come to bring peace to demons or any non-humans. Vexed, stressed out *demons* is not toxicity, that's ministry. Discern if who or what you are "stressing out" is the person or their demons that they've embraced or ignorantly carrying about. Deliverance is needed.

There is nothing in the toxicity definition or symptoms that matches Jesus. Jesus was not toxic, so we should not be either.

Live your life; learn from your experiences. Don't just survive and moan and complain through life. Enjoy it. Do your Earth works, which for most of us, it's probably work we have to do on *ourselves* such as soul prosperity--, which is growing up, maturing, learning, understanding the will of God, the Word of God and doing it. We should be *agape* loving one another.

We sometimes endure traumas. We go through those tests and trials, but they grow us up. We are headed toward godly perfection, beginning with the end in mind.

It is done. In the end, it is done because it's done already.

By done, it's not just the *manner* in which something is accomplished. It's not about the *process* by which it is accomplished, but it is **that** it is done. It is that it is finished. It is completed. It is forever settled in Heaven. It is done.

It is done. So, in this love affair, this great love affair--, the one that you're having with God, and God is having with you, you can honestly say to God, *"You complete me. Lord, thank You for bringing my soul out of captivity, out of bondage, out of toxicity, in the Name of Jesus."*

It is done.

AMEN.

***Dear Reader:**#*

Thank you for acquiring and reading this book. I pray it makes your life better. Soul toxicity is not God's plan for us. May the Lord deliver all who ask and need it, quickly.

Blessings,

Dr. Marlene Miles

Books in this series

Upgrade: How to Get Out of Survival Mode

https://a.co/d/5SZEkcd

Toxic Souls

https://a.co/d/hU1z576

Legacy

https://a.co/d/dDhmoU1

Christian books by this author:

AK: Adventures of the Agape Kid

AMONG SOME THIEVES

As My Soul Prospers

Behave

Churchzilla: The Wanna-Be Bride of Christ

The Coco-So-So Correct Show

Demons Hate Questions

Do Not Orphan Your Seed

Do Not Work for Money

Don't Refuse Me Lord

The FAT Demons

got Money?

Let Me Have a Dollar's Worth

Living for the NOW of God

Lord, Help My Debt

Lose My Location

Made Perfect In Love

The Man Safari *(Really, I'm Just Looking)*

Marriage Ed., *Rules of Engagement & Marriage*

The Motherboard: *Key to Soul Prosperity*

My Life As A Slave

Name Your Seed

Plantation Souls

The Poor Attitudes of Money

Power Money: Nine Times the Tithe

The Power of Wealth

Seasons of Grief

Seasons of War

SOULS in Captivity

Soul Prosperity: Your Health & Your Wealth

The *spirit* of Poverty

The Throne of Grace, *Courtroom Prayers*

Time Is of the Essence

Triangular Powers (4 book series)

    Powers Above

    Sun Block

    Do Not Swear By the Moon

    Star Struck

Upgrade Series
- **How To Get Out of Survival Mode**
- **Toxic Souls**
- **Legacy**

Warfare Prayer Against Poverty

When the Devourer is Rebuked

The Wilderness Romance (3 book series)
- **The Social Wilderness**
- **The Sexual Wilderness**
- **The Spiritual Wilderness**

Other Journals & Devotionals by this author:

The Cool of the Day – Journal *for times spent with God*

got HEALING? Verses for Life

got HOPE? Verses for Life

got WISDOM? Verses for Life

got GRACE? Verses for Life

got JOY? Verses for Life

got PEACE? Verses for Life

got LOVE? Verses for Life

He Hears Us, Prayer Journal *in 4 different colors*

I Have A Star, **Dream Journal** *in styles for kids, teen, young adult and up.*

I Have A Star, **Guided Prayer Journal,** *2 styles: Boy or Girl*

J'ai une Etoile, Journal des Reves

Let Her Dream, Dream Journal *in multiple colors*

Men Shall Dream, Dream Journal, *(blue or black)*

My Favorite Prayers (in 4 styles)

My Sowing Journal (in three different colors)

Tengo una Estrella, Diario de Sueños

Illustrated children's books by this author:

Big Dog (8-book series)

Do Not Say That to Me

Every Apple

Fluff the Clouds

I Love You All Over the World

Imma Dance

The Jump Rope

Kiss the Sun

The Masked Man

Not During a Pandemic

Push the Wind

Tangled Taffy

What If?

Wiggle, Wiggle; Giggle, Giggle

Worry About Yourself

You Did Not Say Goodbye to Me

www.ingramcontent.com/pod-product-compliance
Lightning Source LLC
Chambersburg PA
CBHW061338040426
42444CB00011B/2987